The moment has come

Jabulani R Cele "Ndosi Magaye"

Dedication

I would like to dedicate this writing to life itself for the lessons *it* has taught me. As much as I have gone through so called formal education, life has taught me tremendous lessons that one would not get from any form of education, nor in any of the books from any library or university.

Secondly, I dedicate this to all who have gone through – and to the ones who are still going through – life lessons; the ones who will one day go through them as well as those who avail themselves to support those that are going through life lessons.

Lastly, this work goes to all those who are finding it difficult to support those in need and to those who are finding it hard to move on, following tough life challenges.

I hope that this book facilitates some inner healing and peace of mind while going through what seems to be utter chaos.

Preface

Here are the words from *somebody* who takes himself as a *nobody,* who at the age of nine had to live on the streets of Johannesburg with nothing to rely on but just hope.

A *nobody* who lived in the cracks of his parent's broken relationship and tried to make sense of it. This is a *nobody* who witnessed most of his significant people being swallowed, without forgiveness, by the nowadays' disease.

Here is somebody who knows what it is like to go without food for more than two weeks and still go to school and get to position one in the year-end assessments.

This is somebody who can tell you, without Googling it, what it is like to live in a semi-roofed house at the age of seven and take care of the other sibling coming after him, stretching to make ends meet.

Here are the echoes of the thoughts from a *nobody* who did not learn about witchcraft, *tokoloshes* and *mantindanes* from fairy-tales but who, without understanding it, went through being a victim of it and has had to explain, without being believed, what happened to *normal* people – and got labelled as insane.

Contents

The moment of it happening
to you has come

"It has been happening to others as well."

We live in the space called the world, where there is lots happening. So often, we try to avoid events that we know will be hard to live with. But, no matter how hard we try, the *moment comes* where disaster strikes and we feel like our world is falling apart. When the unpleasant visits your life, it often calls for a change that you are not ready for.

These are the *moments* when you see your life as if it has stopped or is regressing. Life becomes meaningless and you think there has never been a happy moment in your life. All you can see is the event that has happened. You can *feel it, touch it, smell it*, and even *hear it*. It is *the moment* when nothing seems to be real in your life.

To mention just a few of the events that, even though unwelcome, do in the *moment* catch up with us:

- ☹ The death of a loved one.
- ☹ Being diagnosed with a life-threatening disease such as cancer, epilepsy, diabetes, Human Immunodeficiency Virus (HIV), and the like.
- ☹ Rape, assault and physical abuse.
- ☹ Breaking up of a relationship. This may come in the form of either being divorced or dumped.
- ☹ Getting involved in car crash, plane crash, train crash or something similar.
- ☹ Being a victim of violent crime, where your life was threatened and you lost your valuables.
- ☹ Being dismissed from the only job you had when you are the sole breadwinner and have a lot of debts.
- ☹ Learning that our last day is drawing nearer while there is nothing to be done about it.
- ☹ Losing someone close through suicide.
- ☹ Learning that you are going to live with a disability for a long time.

So often, when these moments come they bring along with them disbelief, shock, confusion, feelings of emptiness and a sense of doom. The question is, why is this happening? Why is it happening to me?

Well, I don't know why it is happening but all I know is that *the moment has come for it to happen to you.* Remember that it has happened to others. It is not the first time that it is happening; it has been around, happening to people, real people like you. It has happened to rich and poor, great and small, known and unknown, leaders and followers. To assure you that it has been happening all the time, to different people, amaZulu will tell you *"Akwehlanga lungehli"* or *"Akwehlanga lungehlanga"*, meaning nothing happens that has never happened before. And they don't just say it as a saying because in it there is a serious reminder that it happens and it has happened to others. It also does not mean that you deserve it, but is simply an honest reminder that bad things can happen to anyone.

The fact that it has happened to you at this *moment* has nothing to do with *you.* It has nothing to do with your character, nothing to do with your faith, nothing to do with your sins. The bible pointed it out when Jesus was asked by His disciples as to who sinned for the man to be born blind: was it his parents or himself? The response was it was "neither his parents nor him that sinned, but he is like that so that the works of God may be revealed through him". And according to the story in the bible, the *moment* for that man to see again came (John 9:1).

It has nothing to do with bad luck. It has not happened because someone else asked for it to happen to you. It has not been influenced by someone else's wish. The fact that it hadn't happened before had nothing to do with good luck. Just like a child when it comes to this earth, it just comes. No matter how much it was expected or unexpected; wanted or unwanted.

Events, like children, just come; and often when they are least expected.

It happened because it had to happen and it has been possible for it to happen. Moreover, it has happened because *the moment* for it to happen *has come*. As a result, we are living in the *times* where "cover" – insurance products and policies – are sold to individuals like never before. This cover aims to ease the situation should the unforeseen strike – should *the moment come* – and as a result the business is booming.

Lots of last cents are spent on cover such as life cover, car insurance, house insurance, accidental cover, funeral polices, dread disease cover, disability cover, retirement policies, retrenchment cover, legal cover, even handbag cover. I have not seen one covering individuals for the issues of divorce, though.

We are so covered that in a way we forget that we still have our *today* to enjoy, and should perhaps not be throwing all the last cents we have into covering events we hope will not come. We are so covered that we have no taste for life.

A lot of investment is put into the issues of coping with something when – if – it happens. It seems people are intuitively preparing beforehand, as if they know that there is a great chance of something unpleasant happening. One may register for a course in first-aid, fire-fighting or paramedics, not because one knows that there will be a fire, but in order to be prepared for the tough times when *the moment comes*.

It has been happening to others for a long time; now *the moment has come* that it happens to you. It has a lot more to do with the *moment* than good or bad luck. Even though our actions *may* influence the time factor for the events, the emphasis is on the time, *the moment*.

We know we are all going to die at some stage in our lives, but we don't know the time until the *moment* we actually die.

Likewise, the currently married couple is aware that there is something called divorce, and that others end up experiencing it, but the *moment* will decide and tell whether it will form part of their history or not.

It happens sometimes that one moment comes before another. *The moment* may come while married or when one of the partners is deceased. Maybe you have heard people saying, "If he were still alive, we would have been separated by now. I could see from the way things were happening it was getting worse all the time, no matter what I tried."

There are people who in the presence of HIV never use condoms with their sexual partners but don't get infected with the HI Virus. On the other hand, there are people who got infected with HIV in their very first sexual encounter. It is all a matter of whether *the moment has come* for someone to get infected or not.

There are games that, when one is watching them, one can tell that if the game had gone on a bit longer the other team may well have won instead. In the Olympic Games of 2012 in London, it was easy to see that if the time or distance had been just a minute or a metre more Caster Semenya, a renowned South African female athlete (runner) of this time would have got the first position. It was just a matter of time.

Some moments come before others. For some, their moment of death comes before their moment of divorce, trauma, shame and humiliation, even though those moments were on their way to them. It is just that the moment of death came before other moments, which were still coming. The thing is, no one knows when the moment will come for each one of us.

The *moment will come* that it happens to you, just as the moment came for it to happen to others, and as it will come for it to happen to some in the future. But for now it has been *the moment that it happens to you.*

If you were to be honest, and you had a choice for it to happen to someone else and not you, who would you choose? Why that individual? How do you think that person would think or feel if he were to be told that it happened to him because he was your choice?

The story is told of a guy who complained about the heavy load that he was carrying. Then a voice came from nowhere, asking him to push his heavy load through the door into the hall right in front of him. Having done as he was ordered, he was then asked to go into the hall through the main entrance. Entering the hall, he saw lots of loads. Some were very big; some were medium and two were relatively small.

He was then asked to pick up any load of his choice and leave with it as if it were his own. He chose what he thought was the smallest one and turned to leave. As he firmly put it on his shoulders the voice asked how the new load felt and whether he was sure about his choice. He nodded, saying, "Yes, this is far better and I will go a long way with this one".

As he was leaving the voice said, "That is exactly the load you pushed in through that door there". The load was his and the load is still his.

A friend of mine once said, "We all have problems; it is just that one gets used to one's own problems sometimes. If we could exchange our problems, you would come running back after less than a day, saying, "Please give my problems back to me; I can't cope with yours".

Both good and bad is guaranteed to come to meet us and pass while in this life. This is despite bad and good luck, despite *umuthi* and witchcraft. Therefore, it helps a great deal for one to open one's eyes to be able to see again the good that still exists, when the bad *has come*.

It is important for all of us to understand that with time all shall come and all shall pass.

None of us know why bad things happen to us. Even if we can find our scapegoats and culprits, we still don't know why misfortune chooses us. But we also know that no one is immune from misfortune. The bad and the good catch up with everyone at any given moment. Sometimes it seems we can predict when good or bad is likely to happen, but the truth is nobody knows the exact time. You can only be sure when the moment has actually come for it to happen to you.

It is happening to you because *the moment has come for it to happen to you.* You could not prevent it because the moment has come for it to happen to you. If it were not yet the moment for it to happen, you would be able to prevent it, but it has happened because the moment has come for it to happen.

How can this be happening? Nobody knows, but the moment has come for it to happen. It is in these moments where amaZulu would encourage acceptance by saying *"kusho ukuthi bese kufik'is'khathi sisi..."* meaning *"the time for it has come, my sister"*.

The moment of denial has come

"Denial urges us to look for more detailed facts."

We should give thanks for the gift of denial. Denial is one of our natural automated responses to a situation that may be about to overwhelm us. This is a natural tool we use when something has happened but one unconsciously chooses to believe that it has not happened, regardless of the fact that it really has happened. An example could be when one is diagnosed with HIV and one responds with utterances such as, "No! It can't be", "I don't have HIV", "This is not happening".

I thank the gift of denial because it is a short-term coping mechanism. It prevents us from being overwhelmed by the realities we are not prepared to face, or at least not as yet. It helps us to deal with the realities that we are not yet ready to deal with.

When the bad strikes and we are not yet ready to deal with it, just before one gets overwhelmed denial kicks in, coming to our rescue. When you are told that a person very close to you has died, the most immediate response is something like, "Oh no!" "Don't tell me that!", "It can't be!", "You must be joking," or "Really?"

I like these responses because, while they show disbelief about what has happened, at the same time they beg for confirmation. They then often encourage the messenger, the news breaker, to give more detailed facts about the event, thus giving all the possible evidence to an account. If enough facts are given, it is most likely that the receiver of the news will move on to the following phase, when the *emotions* come into play. It is very important that all the evidence is received and analysed.

Denial shows that we are not passive receptors of information. It is that part of us that is sceptical and seeks to gather more facts before something is accepted as real. I like denial because it serves not only as a short term protective mechanism, but also urges us to research or enquire more, before we accept realities that come with moments.

You may have heard people saying things like "I will only believe it when I see her corpse or bones and have buried them".

The doubting Thomas of the bible did a great job when he said, "I will not believe until I have put my finger into His wounds". Even though the doubting Thomas was criticised and got reprimanded a little bit for being sceptical, it was worth it because, based on the factual information and accepting the current reality, he then fully believed and moved on from the denial phase. He also helped many people to believe and some insight was shared as to who is blessed.

If it were not for Thomas' doubt and his bravery, as he was not shy about his doubts, Jesus would not have given a lesson that the one who believes without having seen proof is blessed. One should also note that there may have been many other silent doubting disciples who would not have had the guts to say it. But thanks to Thomas for respecting his doubts and acting accordingly to help many.

Denial is usually short lived because it is always confronted with concrete evidence that says, "No matter how you wish for something better than this, for now it is *the moment* for you to face that it has happened, and it *has happened to you*". Then, the angles for alternative or preferred scenarios may have crossed your mind are closed as evidence is brought forward. Seeing that there is no other preferred scenario to cling onto, but only our harsh reality that is crystal clear in front of us, denial gives up and leaves.

Generally, denial serves as a short-term coping mechanism and therefore does not last very long. However, it does happen in rare cases that people stay in denial a bit longer. If denial gets to that level, then the moment for seeking some professional help has come, and a psychologist, spiritual leader, counsellor or psychiatrist should be consulted.

The moment has come

If the facts are enough, denial starts to shy away and more coping mechanisms come into play. Then the moment to start doing something about the fact that it has happened and cannot be undone comes.

The moment for mitigations
and bargaining has come!

"We are not passive recipients of
moments that come to us."

There is an *Nguni* proverb: *"Ingane engakhali ifela embelekweni"*. This is interpreted as *"If you don't tell or do something about it, you may die and nobody will have noticed that you have been struggling"*. This is a *moment* that may follow perhaps when one realises that denial has no effect at all in changing the unpleasant reality that one is faced with. It is at this *moment* that one has now learned that one cannot chase away an unpleasant experience by denying it. And when one now realises that there is not enough denial to chase away the miserable situation that one has found oneself in, this is then followed by the moment in which one starts to do something about it.

This moment is marked by *mitigations and bargaining*. When this moment has arrived, one starts to now look back to see if there is any room for *negotiating* one's way out of the unwelcome reality. This may include even praying for the situation to be, if possible, undone or be changed completely.

In this moment, individuals try all they can to *bargain*, *mitigate* and *negotiate* their way out. All the bribery attempts, praying for a miracle to happen, expressions such as, "If I could turn back the hands of time," and "If I could be HIV negative again I would abstain from sex forever," are examples of this moment.

It is in this moment of a striking event that you get an individual who is served with divorce papers saying, "I am sure we can talk about this; can't we talk about it?" What an individual is not aware of is that the truth of the matter is that the reality is here to stay.

Others run to an obviously dead person and shout out his name, not because of the belief that they may be hearing from the spiritual world, but in this case with a hope and faith that the deceased *may* respond. Well, this seems to have worked for the man of great faith who, when the moment of his last day on earth had come, knelt down and asked God if He could remember at least one good deed he may once have done to postpone the death date. We are told that God granted it according to his plea and the death date was postponed, perhaps until further notice.

We should give thanks to this moment of bargaining and mitigation because it serves as a milestone towards acceptance, as one can rightfully say at the end of everything that one has tried all one could try. Doctors, when they come back from the Intensive Care Unit (ICU) to report their failure to change the reality to the loved ones of a deceased, say "We have tried everything…"

It is a moment that once again shows that human beings are not just passive recipients of the realities in their environment, but that they are actively fighting for what they feel they deserve until the end. They try all they can before moving on to accepting the moments as they come. This also shows that we exhaust all the alternatives that may be available before we move onto allowing the next moment to come into play.

*The moment of facing anger, pain,
fear and loneliness has come*

"We fear more if we know less."

When we start to realise that negotiations, mitigation and bargaining are not working, the moment of anger comes. This moment is marked by anger and aggression. One may display episodes of anger ranging from mild to serious. This anger may be directed at self, the carers, objects that are associated with an event, or things that may be associated with the cause of an event. These may be real causes or perceived causes. Sometimes these perceptions may be wrong or inaccurate.

Aggression and anger may be directed even at a supreme being such as God or the ancestors. If it is directed at the spiritual being, it may, sometimes, be in the form of a question such as, "Why did God allow this to happen to me?" or "What wrong have I done to the ancestors to deserve this?"

In this moment it is crucial to know that *good* and *bad* things happen to both *good* and *bad* people. It is also worth knowing that meeting good and bad events in our lives confirms the fact that we are moving forward, we are alive, we are growing and we are going somewhere.

Another interesting fact to note in this moment is that anger is often not the main feeing. I mean, it is not the primary feeling. The main feeling may be another feeling altogether. Anger may result from a feeling of guilt. In this case, one may be angry because one feels it is one's own fault that the event has come to pass. For instance, "It happened because I did not lock the house doors properly; that is why it happened," or maybe, "It happened because I did not take the deceased to the right hospital".

It is worth noting that we cannot be perfect at all times and that this is what makes us human beings.

Another feeling that may be underlying anger is pain. Pain is the feeling that confirms that whatever has happened is not good. It is an emotion that needs expression. People experience and express pain differently. The most common way is through crying. Though crying is perceived differently in different cultures, it remains the healthiest and most effective means of expressing pain. Moreover, crying is normal and it needs not to be suppressed.

In cultures in which crying by certain individuals, such as men, is forbidden, it may be healthy to cry in private places. It has been scientifically proven that individuals who cry when faced with pain cope better than their counterparts who do not.

As much as pain can be as negative as it is, it helps us to focus. It gives us something to feel and thus fosters humbleness in us. And lastly, it gives us the reason to make a way to avoid it in the future or to be more resilient in future should a similar situation come along. In short, it helps us to grow through making us prepare for the future. It is through feeling pain that one learns to behave in a way that will make one feel less pain or no pain in future.

Sometimes, fear may be a proxy for anxiety and uncertainty. Fear comes because we don't know and we are not sure. We don't know what to expect next. We don't know whether to trust again or not in the future. We don't know after an event we really did not like whether or not we still have control over our lives anymore.

The fact that we don't have all the answers triggers a feeling of being overwhelmed and consequently raises fears. Hence the saying, "the less we know the more we fear".

We seem to be more scared of "strangers" than the people we think we know. That will be until the person we think we know does something we never expected, then we start getting worried or fear again because we *don't know* why we thought we knew the person and are now proven wrong.

Then all the fear is compelling us to start asking questions and to start seeking answers for those questions that we did not dare to seek answers for. Questions such as, "How am I going to go on? Is there still hope for me in life? Will I be able to cope? Who can I rely on? Is this passing? Has this ever happened to anyone else? Will I ever be happy again?"

All these questions and similar ones come and go, keeping the brain very busy trying to find answers. Now, when the brain is too busy it will need more energy and more oxygen to work. If more oxygen and glucose is rushing to the brain, it means there will be an increase in the blood flow to the brain. More blood will be travelling in the veins than these veins are used to which now and then puts more pressure on them. This explains the blood pressure and headaches that one may experience sometimes.

When the moments of loneliness and emptiness come into play, they remind us that we are in a moment of fighting, a moment when our strength is being tested, a moment in which we can choose to either break or make our lives.

We should be thankful for the feeling of loneliness for it is through this moment that we tend to focus our thoughts mostly on what has happened. It is a time when we get to reality testing, to try and think more deeply about the moment one is in. It is in diving into this loneliness and emptiness that we get to connect with who we really are. In this moment, we get a chance to be with ourselves.

To make it even stronger, in traditional amaZulu families, during bereavement distractions such as TV-watching and playing of any music from sound systems is discouraged for about a week or, in some places, even a month. This helps the bereaved family to focus on self-healing. It allows time for picking up the pieces that are left and reconnecting them with each other and ultimately allows one to pick oneself up and walk again.

While all these feelings are normal, it is always healthy to become aware of them as they come; to face, express and deal with them. It would also be healthy and good too, to talk to someone professional or indeed anyone that would be able to listen to and support you without judging you, without telling you that you are going to be fine, without trying to dodge the issue and trying to talk you out of the subject.

What is important here is an awareness of how one feels, acknowledgement of one's feelings and expression of them. When the moment of anger comes, it is more important that one finds ways of expressing this without harming any individual. As they say, we all get angry at some stage, but the challenge with it is getting angry with the right person, in the right way, for the right reason, to the right extent and finding the right means of expressing it.

The challenge in this moment is to face anger by finding a healthy way to express it. The most interesting part about the feeling of anger is that it comes with its own energy. Often, this energy comes in order for an individual to be able to use it for fighting or for running away. This is something that those who are learned call the *fight or flight* reaction. This is known as the "double-F" reaction. But nevertheless there is a third "F" that manifests itself by neither flight nor fight, but by a freezing reaction. Some do not fly away, nor fight, but just freeze. That is one of the interesting facts about the way human beings have been created.

Our bodies are tuned to give us what we need when we need it. Likewise, when one deals with an unpleasant situation or is under a stressful situation, the body creates more energy for itself to be able to do more than what it used to do under normal conditions, to compensate for a situation that is no longer normal. That explains the situation in which one says, "I don't know where I got so much power that I was able to surprise even myself".

Now, the question then is, where does this energy go to if the person did not use it for running away (flight) or fighting? Unfortunately, it does not go anywhere. If it does not go anywhere, what does it do to the body? It may start to create some health problems. Does one need medicine to deal with those health problems? Well, it depends. In severe cases, yes, one may need some medical remedies to cope, but the medicinal solutions are short-term and may not be the ultimate solution if the root cause of the problem is not addressed. It should be remembered that these health problems were initially the result of unused energy that is stuck in the body.

One of the recommended ways of dealing with extra energy is finding laborious activities and to "angrily" embark upon them. Sometimes, when dealing with anger it is often recommended that one takes a punch bag and fights it, punching it until one sweats and is feeling nicely tired.

Generally, *fear* is a feeling that feeds, breeds and grows in the lack of knowledge. We now know that it thrives in the absence of accurate information. So, in order to kill it and get done with it once and for all, it helps to start seeking knowledge, joining support groups, and looking for and talking to people who have gone through similar situations and seem to be coping well.

And, in the *moment* of *pain* it helps to know that our bodies are self-healing. It has been proven that our bodies secrete endorphins when we are in pain. Endorphins are hormones that help us to feel the pain as little as possible. It is important, however, to seek medical attention for severe physical pain.

The moment of depression has come

**"Depression forces us to focus even
more and fosters humbleness."**

The feeling of pain, fear and loneliness may bring a moment in which one starts to slow down, talk very little and softly; to look downward, as if dancing to a new tune. At this moment one starts thinking deeply and as far as possible about what happened or what is happening.

We should give thanks to the gift of depression for it helps us *focus even more* on what happened. When the moment of depression comes, it pushes our focus to the maximum. In our day-to-day lives we do focus according to ourselves, but our minds are still busy dealing with other matters that are not actually related to one *single* matter. I thank this moment for it is because of its severity; one's body, mind and soul come together to strengthen each other and to know each other better.

It is after surviving threatening moments that we get to understand ourselves better. It is in this moment when one feels like what is captured in the following poem by J. Cele:

FLIGHTS OF LIGHTS: 2012

Dying Silently
While creating and sustaining the name
While helping the lame is the game
Then the next one comes for you to "save"
Till you see that helping isn't the fame but the shame
And dying silently is the name of the game

Even if it cannot be bio-physiologically found
A psychologist says it is profound
It is a desert where there is no sound
And it can't make even an imbecile proud
It is a condition where you know you are bound
Dying silently makes even the silence loud

And given the individual differences that exist amongst people, some may do the opposite, increasing the pace at which they are doing things and heightening their performance; a condition popularly known as hyperactivity. But still, for healing to take place a slow pace, focus and allowing oneself to go through the situation rather than suppressing it, would be better.

Depression is one of the amazing gifts we get from the experiences that are unpleasant in our lives. Depression helps us to focus mostly on ourselves and what happened or what we are still going through. It teaches us more about an event and also ourselves in a way that, after it, when we have managed to get through it, we become more at peace with what happened and with ourselves. In this moment the brain seems to be looking for no distractions as it is doing its best to integrate what has happened in one's life.

It is this moment that separates survivors from victims.

The moment of acceptance has come

"Life begins with acceptance."

Having realised that it has happened – and no matter how much one might wish to have avoided the moment in which it happened – following all the denials, bargains and mitigations depression and anger, there comes a moment for one to *accept* that it has happened. At this stage it is very important to realise that it has *already happened,* as opposed to thinking that it is happening. The fact that "it happened" is in the past tense remarks that it has passed. Or, put differently, it belongs to the past.

There is very little, if anything, that one can do about what is in the past. Therefore, it is very important to note that the past has passed and gone forever and that as a result one cannot live in the past or cannot have any influence on the things that belong to the past. What is in the past becomes a story, it is called *history,* thus remarking that it can only be told as *"his story"*. Therefore, it would be wiser for one to invest in the today, since whatever one does today is making a new history. One's today need not be spoiled by what happened yesterday, One's today is a *gift*, and maybe that is why it is called the *present*.

What determines whether one will live longer and survive living with the HI Virus has been in most cases the acceptance of the fact that one lives with it and it cannot be changed (at least at the *moment*). The ones who did not survive living with the virus have been in most cases the ones who did not attain any level of acceptance.

The fact that HIV is not accepted prevents one from finding ways to live with it, which consequently lead to a rapid compromise in one's immune system, thus exposing one to opportunistic infections, creating a condition that will be later on be labelled as AIDS. In contrast, those who have accepted the fact that the *moment* for them to live with the virus *has come*, have been found to survive longer.

Acceptance acts as a milestone that, if reached, means one can then start to live life to the fullest with what one is left with. In most of the cases, we tend to focus so much on and put all our efforts into what we have lost. In this way we lose sight of all that we have left in our lives.

Whatever has not been accepted drains a lot of energy from one. The popular Serenity Prayer indicates this, saying, "God, grant me the serenity to *accept* the things I cannot change, *courage* to change the things I can and the *wisdom* to know the difference".

In this prayer we ask to *accept* with peace the things that we cannot change, history being one of them. And the courage to change the things we *can* change. For me, that is asking not to be just passive about the things that life throws at us, but to do something to change what we *can*, which can mostly be the *present*, the status quo.

But the most important part of this prayer is the *wisdom* to know the *difference*. It takes growth and a bit of wisdom to differentiate between the two. It needs extra wisdom to understand that one cannot change the contents of the past but can do better by *accepting* it as the *moment* that came and passed.

The moment of growth has come

**"Today we are making history out of
what was yesterday's future plan."**

AmaZulu would say *"Akuqhawe lingalwanga"*, which teaches one that "there is no hero without going through a fight". Some say, "What does not break you makes you stronger". I say, there is no situation that one can go through and remain the same.

These three phrases illuminate our minds to start seeing that there is growth in suffering and in struggles. Or, to put it differently, the unpleasant events we meet are maybe just a test for us to pass, so as to pass onto another level in our lives. Difficulties just come in the form of an initiation rite. This means that, if we go through the test and pass it, we gain more insight into what life is about.

All the heroes one can count today are called heroes because of the tests they had to pass at some stage in their lives. They are called heroes even if they had to die, *passing* away in the process instead of *passing* the test. Among those who died, one can count in South Africa names such as Steve Biko, Robert Sobukwe, Chris Hani, Tsietsi Mashinini and many more others. Heroes who died internationally include Martin Luther King Jr., for Christians, Jesus the Nazarene, known nowadays as the Christ, and Simon Peter the apostle. And there are, of course, those who survived to tell their story such as Nelson Mandela, a South African poet called Mzwakhe Mbuli and many more.

It is through hardship and humiliation that one's strength is tested and affirmed. It is as if in the events one is transformed. It is hard to go through difficult situations and be the same afterwards. Nelson Mandela's heroism is meaningless without twenty-seven years in jail. Jesus' gospel will have no taste without His passion and crucifixion. King Shaka's story would be boring without the suffering he had to go through with his mother as he grew up. Bantu Steve Biko, and other revolutionary heroes' stories would have been only another story if their way had been just a wide open highway.

What moves individuals whenever their story is shared is the toughness of the journey they had to go through. Some of these heroes are still called heroes even if they were brutally killed on their way to becoming heroes.

After an event is faced and experienced, then the *moment of growth* comes in. It is interesting to know that when challenging situations come, they may be coming in order for us to climb on top of them, thus ending on another level in life.

It is up to you to decide, when life throws dust and stones at you, whether you want to lie down and let the dust and stones form a grave over you or if you are going to shake yourself off and stamp on it to form a hill that lifts you up to tell the good story at the end. You may not choose the moment you find yourself in, but you can choose what you make of it, and the story you make of it. As they say: the choice is yours.

A lot of people have decided to lie down and cling onto the moment and have never wanted to grow up and move on. They become too comfortable with what happened, rather than telling the moment what they want to see happening.

Human beings with potential just decided to become perfect engineers of self-destructive stories. You talk to someone who was a smart classmate, always in the top ten. Then fifteen years later you find him stuck in drugs, poverty and alcohol. You ask about this and you will get good novels about why he could not make it, and he can't make it even in the future since the divorce of his parents, since she was raped, since he was kicked out of his only job, ever since his parents died. *Hhayi bo*! The thing is, your parents are not dying: they have died. It belongs to the past, so grow up.

I grew up hearing phrases such as *"uyakhula"* (you are growing up) whenever I fell, which of course puzzled me every time I heard it. This phrase followed me until the point where I went to pick up a dying lady, who eventually died on my hands while doing so. When I came back I told the story of how the lady died after putting her head on the pillow and I confirmed with her whether I had put her head the way she wanted on the pillow, and she said, "Yes and thank you," closed her eyes and died. Sibongile Sibisi (one of the hospice caregivers) said *"usukhulile-ke"* (you have now grown up).

I failed to understand this until later when I heard about something called post traumatic growth. I was like, "post traumatic what?"

The German educational psychologist Mullman said "growth". What this is all about is the fact that after every traumatic experience we learn new lessons; we find new ways to live on and to adapt. We learn to welcome the change that is posed by the events in our lives.

Observation of life will tell us that the gold takes its beauty from the furnace of fire. Dr Nelson Mandela got his reputation from the years he had to spend in jail and the humiliation he had to go through in there. The bible records that Jesus, too, had to go to His throne via the crucifixion which He did not want. He symbolically indicated it as drinking from the cup He never wanted to drink from. As far as His "will" was concerned, He declared "…but let Your [God's] will be done".

So what are "tough times" in life if they are not just a test or just a passage that is only there to bring about a survivor as opposed to a victim – a better individual, a graduate, or should I say an initiate afterwards? When amaZulu say, *"Indlela ibuzwa kwabaphambili"* (literally meaning, "You ask for the directions from the ones who are ahead of you") they are actually saying, if you are struggling with it, ask for advice from the ones who have been there and passed. See the emphasis that those who *have been through it* are actually ahead (*phambili*). Why ahead? They are ahead in knowing and experiencing the situation that you are currently struggling with. They have *grown* in knowing how to do it.

Let's take the example of someone who is living with HIV. At this *moment* one has grown into understanding many areas of living with HIV in a way that one can now mentor the newcomers living with HIV. That is why the concept of support groups has tremendous value when it comes to supporting those who are going through an unwelcome situation in life. The value comes with the fact that it includes individuals who have been there, have gained some control and expertise over the situation and now can share with others as to how they are coping.

The question is, "How do you get a strong muscle?" An answer is, "You don't buy it from a supermarket but gain it through hard labour or tough exercise". For a muscle to be stronger one has to challenge it by giving it harder jobs to execute. It has to go through pain and endure it for a specific time for it to grow. Like a muscle, one grows through pain and humiliation.

The story is told of a nature lover who saw a butterfly that was struggling to come out of its cocoon. As someone who loves nature, the Good Samaritan in him wanted to do something to help. He went down and reached out to it. He gently pulled the butterfly out of its own cocoon. "There you go," he said. He put the "rescued" butterfly onto the grass so that it could take off from the grass for its first flight. He then went on down the road.

On his way back, he fell down and cried when he noticed that the butterfly he had "rescued" never made it to the sky, but had died on the ground for ants to make a feast out of it.

What went wrong there? The muscles that join the butterfly and its wings were too weak for the butterfly to make successful, stronger flaps for it to fly. These muscles were only going to be strengthened and grow by the flapping of the wings as the butterfly *struggled* to come out of the cocoon. The *struggle* was essential. That struggle was going to bring about the necessary growth. No matter how you look at it, even though going through pain is painful, there is growth in going through pain and a humbling wisdom is gained.

It is part of growth for one to start seeing life after turmoil and disaster. It is for the grown-ups to realise that, even in a seriously bad situation, life continues and that one can live with the changes and that there are valuable lessons to be learned from that experience.

While there is consensus that all normal human beings have two eyes, I dare to think that one has more than two eyes. Otherwise, people who are known as *blind* would not say, "*Oh, I see,*" at any stage of their conversation in their lifetime. Likewise, it would be very hard to conceive what is being talked about in the bible's book of revelation, as it records that John repeatedly mentioned "*I saw*", while it has been previously mentioned that he had been through an experience that is said to have left him as a *blind man.*

All in all, I dare to believe that one has five or even more eyes and seeing is beyond using only what is known as the *naked eye.* These five "eyes" take their work depending on the level of growth that an individual may have attained.

The first eyes are the ones that we use to see. These are biological organs that are for the sense of *sight,* but are nevertheless not enough for *insight,* or should I say "*in-sight*"? These are the ones you use to look at this book. These are the eyes that are capable of seeing the people around you and that you use to conclude whether you like them or not, just by looking at them. These eyes are opened the minute one is delivered onto this earth.

Then, the second eyes are *literacy* eyes. These are the eyes you use to see what is written in this book and make sense of it. If these eyes were not opened you would not be able to see what is written in this book. You would see the words, but would not be able to *see* the *sense* they are trying to make. At some stage of growth these eyes get opened and one starts seeing what the written words mean and to *see* the *sense* in them. Added to this is another set of eyes, these are the eyes needed to see symbols. A lot is being communicated through symbols. It takes eyes that can read symbols to see what the symbols are saying. For an example, a cross would mean Christian faith, but this also depends on the type of cross as well.

The third eyes are the eyes of faith. These are the eyes that one uses to see the things that one trusts exist. It is these eyes that believers use to see in the spiritual world and to be sure of the things that have not been confirmed to exist, at least not as yet. It is this type of eyes that perhaps John of the bible used when he was blind on the island of Patmos as he was writing the book of revelations. As much as he was declared blind at that time, he kept on saying, "Then I saw…, and I saw…", and most of what he wrote was then taken as a true reflection of the times to come and of what the heavens are like. The same eyes may have been used *more clearly* by the prophets as they often have claims of seeing things from different worlds. It takes a certain level of growth for these eyes to open up and function.

The fourth eyes are the ones that one uses to see what another person is seeing. So often people fight simply because they don't *see* the same point as the other *sees* it. The fact that it is the same point that is being looked at doesn't matter. We have so many religions and even within the same religious belief such as Christianity there is still a grave division amongst Christians themselves; hence the countless denominations that even today are still mushrooming – and this will continue for as long as *bengasaboni ngasolinye* (literally meaning they no longer *see with one eye*).

Perhaps it is the role of these eyes to see what the other is seeing. If these eyes are not opened, divisions are guaranteed to result. They serve a purpose of seeing what the other is seeing. If these eyes are open, you become content and live with others peacefully, because you are able to see what someone else is seeing and be at peace with it, no matter how different what he sees is from what you see. As mentioned before, these eyes get opened through growth and growth creeps in when these eyes are being opened.

Lastly, the fifth eyes are the ones that we use to see hope in a hopeless situation. These eyes are the ones that are very dangerous if not opened because, like a biologically blind person, one will *see* nothing following a disaster. For such a person, it all becomes dark and he cannot *see* anything at all except darkness. For that person, life becomes so dark and scary that he feels not able to *go on,* simply because it is so dark he cannot *see* where to put his foot for the first step to be taken.

As a result, he may feel life is worth nothing and start having suicidal thoughts. It is through the use of these eyes that people start seeing that there is life beyond being diagnosed with HIV; there is life beyond divorce; there is life even after the death of a loved one; and that there is life even after amputation of one's limb/s, there is life after loss of one's front teeth and that there is life even after the death of self.

These *eyes* help us to *see* life even beyond our wrong doings – or sins, if you like. We see life beyond our shame, guilt and fears. These eyes open up with growth and maturity. They are the ones that help us see hope when most of the people see none. When these eyes are opened, one starts seeing that there is life behind the darkness brought by the events through moments to us.

It is for the grown-ups to see and accept the fact that there are things that need to happen, no matter how bad they may be, for the good things to come along.

When I was asked to talk on the opening of a new building built following one that was tragically burnt down, killing thirty children instantly, I said the old one *had* to go to ashes.

This seemed to shock everyone at the time. But, I went on to say that, for this structure, beautiful as it was in front of us on that day, to be built, the old one had to cease to exist. This means that the old one was standing in the way of this newly-built beautiful structure.

As much as the experience that caused it to go was horrific, it had to happen in order for this beauty to come out. It is the same when it comes to the story of Jesus. According to the bible, as cruel as the way He died was, it had to be so in order for Christians to claim salvation. It is even puzzling that the Friday that Jesus is said to have been crucified is called "good Friday". Note the "good" part of it. Go to Christians and they will tell you why the killing of a Jew who was supposed to bring hope and lead Jews to a state of peace (Shalom) is taken as "good".

There is often the bad that has to happen for more good to come about. One goes around covered by policies that promise money that one may never even get in one's lifetime. However, as much as one's death would be distasteful to most, so much will be achieved following it by one's significant others. The policy companies often promise to even double the price should death result from an accident.

I said "death by an accident". But nevertheless it is for the grown-ups and for the ones with the fifth eye opened to see life

The moment has come

even in horrific situations. It is these eyes that the psycho-social professionals and counsellors are trying to open for individuals in the face of adversities. When these eyes are open, and life is seen beyond the disaster, then growth is achieved.

The moment of ritualising and commemoration has come

"Rituals leave monuments behind them."

S ome of us who took care of cows and milked them will know that a cow becomes so habituated to the process and experience of being milked that, after milking her one needs to pat the cow on the back, to sort of say to her, "It is over now; you can move on".

That is for helping someone who still says, "Ever since my mother died things never went back to their normal state," or "Ever since I got divorced my life became a mess".

In most cases, one can deduce that this person is still living what happened as if it is still happening, even today and now. It triggers one to respond with such phrases as, "You have been divorced since that date and that year, *that moment* and not today; you are not getting divorced now". That *moment* of being divorced has come and gone. One has to actually see that the moment has come and to let go of that moment so that it is now gone – and to see that there is no need to live in it anymore.

When one is able to see that the particular moment is gone and another one has come, it is at that moment when one is able to perform the necessary and relevant rituals.

In my neighbourhood in the early 1990s I witnessed a case where a most beloved daughter of someone welcomed a moment of death when it came. On the other hand, her mother was not so ready for that moment. She preferred to have her daughter around, for her to continue talking to her, solving their day-to-day problems as they came. However, the truth was that that moment was gone as far as the reality was concerned. As a result, the moment to do even the first ritual (the funeral) that accompanies death was not welcome.

The mother went ahead, welcoming women from the village who came to her house to express their condolences, but she did so while living in the moment of denial for the whole five weeks, telling whoever visited that her daughter was very tired and therefore sleeping, but she would eventually wake up.

That was until the smell from her decomposing daughter's corpse was strong enough to tell her that the *moment* for her to start grieving had come. It was only then that she saw that the moment for her to be with her daughter had come and gone, and now was the moment to begin with relevant rituals necessary for the funeral.

Rituals are the activities that we do to indicate that, whatever it is that has happened, it now belongs to the past. Rituals act as indicators or yardsticks that separate the moments that belong to the past and the present, as we prepare for the future. They help us to separate the moments and appreciate them as we clearly and rightfully put them where they belong, which is in the past. They help us not to mix the moments, which often come with distress and thus malfunctioning.

Remembering what is in the past is healthy, but living in the past as if it is happening today cripples the appreciation of the present moment. Remember what happened in the past, but do not live in it as if it is happening today. Draw strength from the past and never let the past drain your energy today.

Rituals can take any form. You may be aware that there are a lot of traditional, unique or cultural rituals. Traditional rituals are the ones that are always expected to follow after a particular event. For instance, the funeral must always follow after the death of a normal human being as a ritual.

Unique rituals often follow unique events. An example would be in a traditional Zulu family where, if the cause of death is from an accident, there are extra special rituals to prevent the misfortune repeating itself.

Culture is a way of life, and customary and cultural rituals are the rituals that contain in them some prescriptions. These rituals sort of detail what to do when a specific event has happened and how one goes about doing rituals around that event. I will continue with the example of death by an accident. According to the culture of amaZulu, the corpse is never allowed to come to the home. The whole funeral is held outside the gate of the family but nearby the premises of the deceased. This is believed to prevent similar incidents from happening again in the future – what is known as *umkhokha*.

It does not matter the kind of rituals being done, but whenever they are done they help the ones who are participating in them to focus on what has happened and rightfully put an event that has happened to where it belongs, which is the past.

When rituals are performed they often leave a symbol behind them, the *monument*. The crosses with flowers, similar to those that are often seen in graveyards, are the symbols of rituals. When one sees those symbols on the roadside, the thought of an unpleasant event that might have occurred there crosses one's mind. One thinks to oneself, "Something has *happened* here". Note that the phrase is usually in the past tense. The past tense indicates that whatever it was that happened there belongs to the past. One never thinks, "Something *is happening* here", but rather something *has happened* there. That is how instrumental the rituals are in separating the moments. They are there to tell a story that something has happened here.

The graves too are an example of the symbols of an event of death that would already have occurred. Graves are saying, "Someone has died and was put to rest here". On the same note they tell of what happened and not what is happening. In that manner the rituals have that power to separate the moments.

Likewise, the horns of a slaughtered cow are put on top of a thatched house, upon an entrance, not to boast to people passing by that this home could afford to slaughter a whole big cow one day, but as a symbolic monument of a ritual.

Even the red HIV and AIDS ribbon acts as a symbol, indicating *moments* that came and got accepted at some stage. That is from the *moment* of denying the existence of the HI virus to trying to do something about it and hoping for the best in future. The big red symbol of AIDS found outside the Worksop in Durban in Gugu Dlamini Park is not just there for decoration. It tells a story of a young lady who was stoned to death following her public declaration that she was living with the then most denied virus, HI. And the park was then named after her because of her heroic act and her courage in coming out and disclosing her HIV status in a community that was not so ready to accept the severity of AIDS.

All these symbols are therefore there to help the survivors to acknowledge the *moment* that *came* and also that it belongs to the past. Those symbols tell a story that the survivors have done something to *accept* the *moment* and have acknowledged that it has happened, as opposed to thinking that it is still happening. These symbols often trigger a chain of thoughts and questions to those not involved. Whenever these ritualistic symbols are seen by the non-witnesses of *the moment* of a particular event, intuition just starts feeding their senses that these monuments are standing there to tell a story. They say, "Something has happened here".

"The taste of a story is in the severity
of the challenges in it."

After each and every event that life throws at humanity, heroes come out. The tougher the conditions we go through in life, the stronger the heroes that come out. Even if some of the heroes die in the process, as a result of the toughness of the conditions, the honour is still given to them as fallen heroes. When one visits any of the museums on the globe the story of the heroes comes alive and heroism takes its honour.

There is no story that is as boring as that of a man that is told as: Mr Cele was born, lived life like any other normal person and died. On hearing such as story one goes, "And then…?"

And then one wonders whether it was even worth talking about that person. It is so because of the fact that there is no story in that narration. But when it comes to individuals who were confronted with huge events and challenges, like King of amaZulu, uShaka kaSenzangakhona, Jesus (Yehoshua) who the bible says is of Nazareth, Dr Nelson Rholihlahla Mandela, Bantu Steve Biko, Martin Luther King, Robert Sobukwe, and many more, you may think *and then*, and then the story becomes even more interesting. What breathes life into the story is the devastating events, challenges and the sometimes "seems to be impossible" *moments* that they had to allow themselves to go through when the *moment came*.

It is interesting to observe that most of the inspiring poets that I know of, the book authors that I am aware of, and most of the best artists I know of, are products of unpleasant life events and their artistic craft is often mostly influenced by the tough moments they have been through.

When one reads any novel that is based on a true story, one gets encouraged by how the characters (more especially the main character) in the story dealt with the issues that they are confronted with. The tougher the situations, the more interesting and encouraging the story becomes. When I read *Cry Freedom*, a book about Bantu Steve Biko, one of the South African fallen heroes of the apartheid struggle, it was the first time that I read and finished a book in twelve hours.

It is a pity though that there are multitudes of heroes who die with their stories untold. That is the case even in the days of advanced technology which one can use to tell one's story.

As they say, a bell is never a bell until the bell rings and a story is not a story until it is told. It is saddening to know that most people have their heroic stories dying untold within themselves. It has been proven that when a story is told, the story loses its control over an individual because it no longer stays in an individual's subconscious mind, where it has power to influence an individual's behaviour unconsciously. When the story is told, it loses its power over the person and the person regains his power over the story that used to be untold and hovering around above him, threatening him and holding him back. Perhaps that is why people are encouraged from left, right, centre, bottom and above to break the silence and start talking after they have been victimised in order for them to come out as survivors.

The telling of the story helps an individual to offload and as a result become freer than is the case when the story is not told.

The people who have been exposed to the churches where a believer is offered an opportunity to "confess" his "sins" in the presence of a priest or a chaplain are aware of an experience of freedom that is felt after the process of opening up and telling the story. This freedom is real because of the fact that the story that is untold has power to haunt and belittle the individual affected by it. It keeps on holding the individual back, reducing self-confidence to almost zero.

When the story is being told you can notice that the listeners are changing the mood and the emotions with the story being told. This comes from the fact that the "storyteller" is offloading by telling the story and thus allowing the listener or listeners to share the load that has been carried by the storyteller alone.

One may remember that those who cope better, as far as living with the HI virus is concerned, are those who disclose their HIV status and start to openly talk about the heroic moments that come and go as they continue with their journey of living with HIV. Talking about it brings back control over it and ultimately over one's life. It also helps others confronted with the similar moment to cope better.

It is also worth noting that a story that has never been told has more control over the individual who keeps it as a secret; hence the saying that secrets kill. Moreover, untold experiences have power to control us because what has been experienced has never been given a name, and thus serves as an unknown *demon*. What then heals in telling the story is the fact that one starts giving names and *labels* to what happened and thus gains control over what was an unnamed experience.

aMazulu would say, "*Ith'ingabankulu ingabe isazekeka,*" which directly translates as "the bigger the event becomes, the harder it becomes to talk about it". This shows that the power of the encounter grows with an inability to talk about it and the untold story controls the individual.

However, when one tries to talk about it, in the process one starts to find words for it and to give names and labels to what happened, and this drains power from the unnamed demon.

It is only when what happened can be named that one starts to gain control over what happened. For those who read the bible not only as a religious book, it is interesting to note that the bible records that Jesus struggled to expel the demons from the man who is said to have been living in the graveyard. He struggled until He asked for the name of the demon, and the demons in the man knew Him, and responded to Him with their name. It was only when the demons disclosed their name as Legion (and added that they called so because they are many) that He was able to expel them. The power here is in naming and controlling.

There are so many ways in which heroes do their storytelling when the moment to tell their story comes. Some discover that they can tell their stories through music, whereby songs are written and sung. One would note that in these days the more emotions you put in the story the more your song will sell in South Africa. If the story or a song looks sad and appeals to other emotions, one can be sure that the art will touch many hearts.

One can put forward powerful artists such as Donny Ngwenyama, the singer of *"Basheshe bahleka kanti iNkosi ikuzwile"*, " *Kulungile*" by a gospel singer Sifiso Ncwane, "Lean on me" by Kirk Franklin and many more. You will notice this in the genres such as *Umaskandi,* (a word which evolved from a Dutch *musikant,* meaning a musician), a South African isiZulu traditional music. As an example, some will recall how the song by Shwi Nomtekhala titled *"Ngafa"* (I am dying) sold triple platinum in a year and got awards, while it was just about a man miserably complaining about dying of an illness he suspected having acquired from his *"unfaithful"* sexual partners.

In the gospel music genre, one may recall the music of Dr Rebecca Malope, who got an honorary doctorate and a title of Queen of Gospel music through her gift of being able to artistically tell painful stories through her music – and also her exceptional talent in acting them out.

Some become prominent poets while yet others do well in telling their story through painting and pottery. Some just decide to write it down in the form of a novel or a short story. Some make films and theatre plays with their stories. Life is about making stories and telling those stories to others to help them live better. As the moment passes, stories become history.

The moment of telling the story has come. Tell yours, it is worth telling.

As long as there is a listening ear – a listening and not just a hearing ear – go ahead and tell your story.

When the story is told it needs no evaluation, no moralising and no judgement.

If they want to judge, let them judge and be judged.

Cross the frontiers and break the barriers. Come out of the dark cave and tell your story.

Break out of your shell and tell your story.

If other people think there are some wrong things, who cares? Let them care and care less, as you share your story.

…And feel the relief

WHEN THE TIME COMES…

When my eyes have
Stopped winking
Tell the world it was
Too much for them

When my eyes have
Stopped seeing
Tell them they
Have seen a lot

When my mouth
Has stopped talking
Say it was a
Speechless encounter

When my mind
Is no longer
Working, inform
Them it overworked

When my hands
Can't move anymore
Let them know they
Couldn't handle it

When my ears
Can no longer hear
Tell them they
Have heard it all

Jabulani Cele "Ndosi Magaye"

When I can't feel
Anymore
Let everyone know
That I've felt enough

When anyone thinks
Of crying tell that one
Crying didn't help me,
Sometimes it doesn't help

When anyone asks
Why it had to be like
This
Say I myself
Ask the same

When my legs have
Stopped walking
Say there was too
Much wailing already done
So they decided to end the journey.

When my nose and
Lungs have stopped
Breathing tell them
It was all
breathtaking.

AS YOU SEE ME THERE!

Come there and see me there,
Come to the street and see me there.
Don't look at me,
But look for me.

Oh, dear! Are you so blind?
So blind that you can't see me
Beyond these dirty filthy clothes
Behind these ragged clothes?

If you look beyond this dirt, there is me,
Under this "Kaffir haar" there is me.
In here there is me searching.
There is me with a story.
The story of my life.

You may call me a street kid
If you want to,
But what are you?
Is your stereotype solid enough,
Enough to blindfold you?

My friend, how did you contribute
To me being here?
I will remain here till you wake up.
I do have mind, blood and brain
I had, and still have life.

Don't assume I am hungry for food.
Your care, love, understanding,
Your respect and reconstruction
Is what I desire.
Truly, inside "that street kid", there is *me*.

If you have eyes, why don't you see me?
If you have ears, why can't you hear me?
If you have a mouth, can't you talk to me?
To me and not about me.

If you have love and care, are you really
Intending to keep it to yourself and
Think you are free from blame and guilt?
Who are you, then?
Or should I say, what are you, then?
Who do you work for?
Why do you live?

Till when are you going to be like this?
Where are your emotions and
Where is your heart?
Where is your heart?
Have a heart and then come.
Come and meet me there.
I live here.
I cry here.

See a street kid in me,
I see more in you.
I see a lot in you.
Till you wake up,
And notice a thing in me.

Maybe you know
Roads were meant for cars,
So it's tough here

Sometimes I am scared
And nobody cares
Never mind the scars
You see in me
You may be scared
And miss the scars
On my soul

When you get to that beautifully-built holy place
Tell them I live here, in these streets
Say hi to your holy book.
You may pray if you want to,
Praise the Lord for you aren't here.
Say hi to the men in front there,
Tell your God again that
God is love.
God bless you, house person,
I am just a kid on the street you saw.

If I Had to Choose 1

If I had to choose
If had a choice
Only if I were to have a say.

I was not going to
Allow myself to be
A subject of poverty
Alleviation project
A platform on which
People alleviate their own
Poverty through mine.

Only if I had a say
I was not going to be
A *Bantu* education student
In apartheid and a segregated
Country
Getting crumbs of education.

Only if I were to have a say
I would have my mum
Close to me
Caring for me
Nurturing me
And not have her
Giving away my
Naturally earned care
To someone else's children

In the city
Somewhere in the suburbs

Only if I had to choose
I would not have to
Start my life as a street child
I would have my mother
Seen as a mother
And my father as a father
Rather than *Jane* a *kitchen-girl*
And *Pikinini* a garden-*boy*
By someone of their children's age

If I had to choose
I would stay somewhere
Better than this
Rain-collecting and
Wind-dancing slum
With no traces of life,
But only smelling of poverty.

Only if I had to choose my fate.

Influences on the writing

As far as there was no direct reference used at the time of writing, I would like to **acknowledge** some of sources of influence that may have had an impact on how this book ended up being written.

1. The title is an isiZulu translated expression "*Kufike isikhathi*", often uttered when consoling the bereaved.
2. The structuring of the first five topics was influenced by the work of Dr Kubler Röss – *the stages of death*.
3. Inclusion of a topic on rituals was influenced by *trauma counselling course* by G-Pellen-Klingler and Silke Mallmann Mmachman of Switzerland and Austria University respectively.
4. A different perspective on the manifestation of traumatic events is inspired by *stress and trauma course* by Dr Carol of St Augustine University in Johannesburg South Africa.

Some of the influence comes from more than ten years of *experience of counselling* individuals who have experienced traumatic and painful events and in fifteen years in HIV and AIDS work.